AF484663

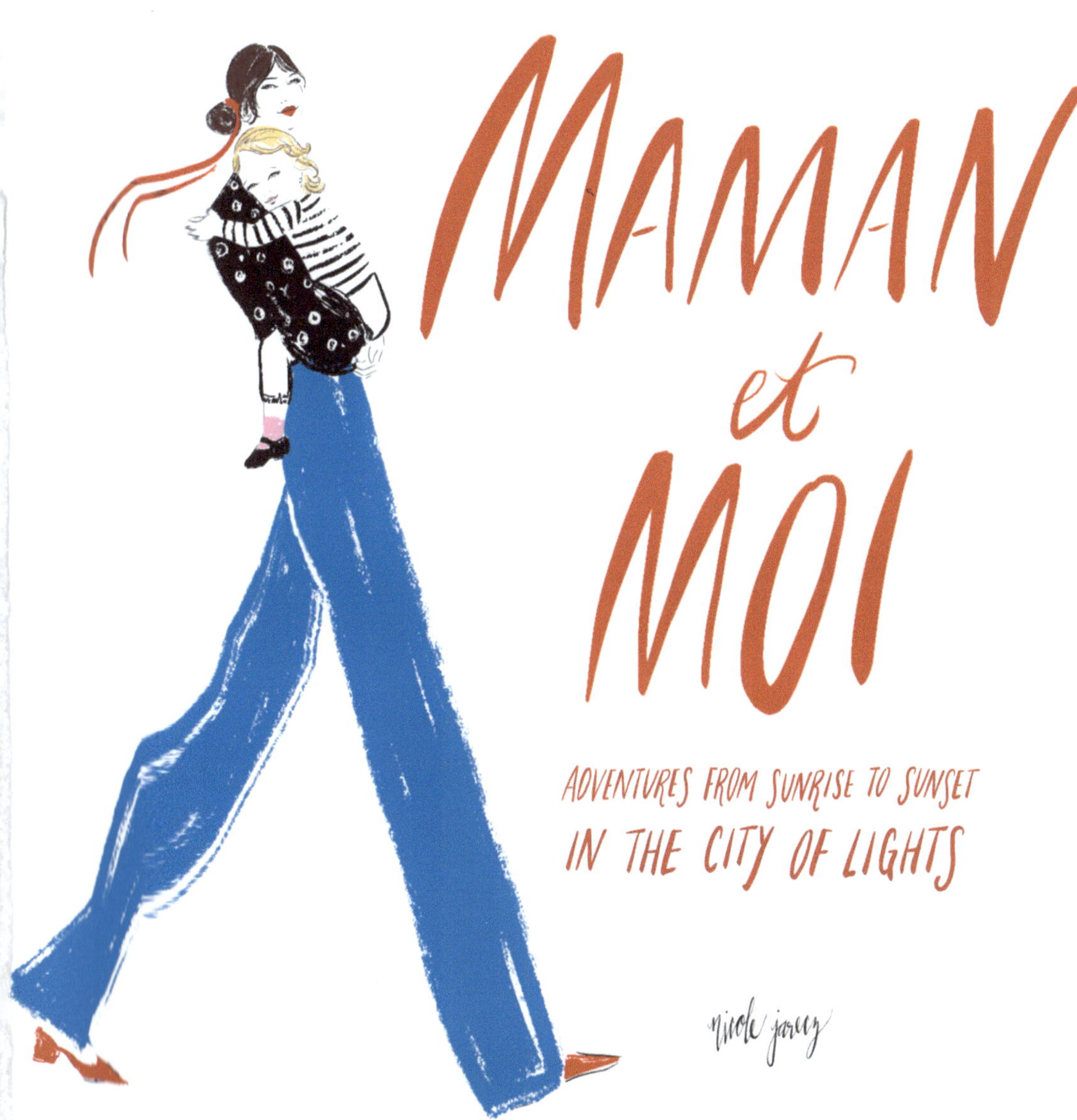

MAMAN et MOI

ADVENTURES FROM SUNRISE TO SUNSET
IN THE CITY OF LIGHTS

nicole jones

For my daughters, Ella and Claire -
my life's greatest adventure

"Good morning!" says Maman as she opens the shutters.
It's time for a *petit-déjeuner[1]* of tartines and butter.

Every Maman in Paris has a different plan for the day.
But there's always room to wander every which way.

[1]*Breakfast*

—Bonjour!

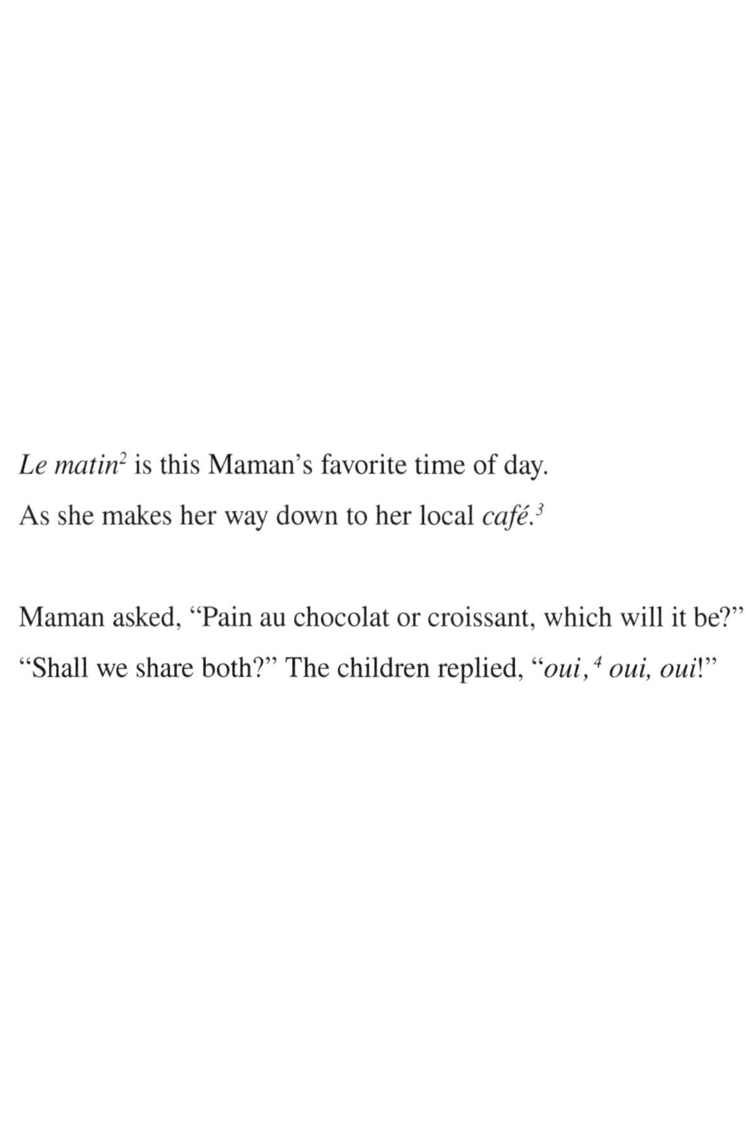

Le matin[2] is this Maman's favorite time of day.

As she makes her way down to her local *café.*[3]

Maman asked, "Pain au chocolat or croissant, which will it be?"

"Shall we share both?" The children replied, "*oui,*[4] *oui, oui*!"

RUE SAINT HONORÉ
CAFE
BAR

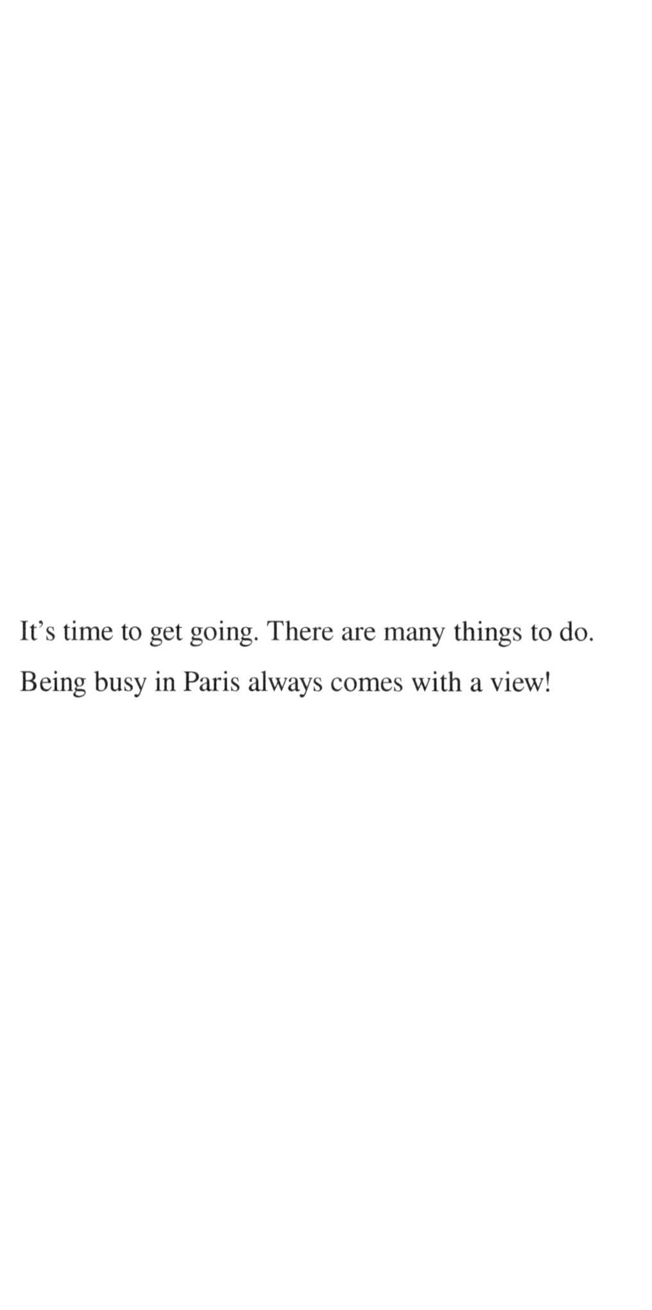

It's time to get going. There are many things to do.

Being busy in Paris always comes with a view!

Place
CHARLES DE GAULLE

We head to our local *marché,*[5] basket in hand

Where colorful produce is very in demand.

CAROTTES
CITRONS
TOMATES
COURGETTES

Our morning *promenade*[6] lasted for hours...

till finally we passed by the Eiffel Tower!

[6]*Walk*

L'APRÈS-MIDI

Where had the time gone? It's already the afternoon.

The children are hungry. Maman says, "we will eat soon."

We found a spot on the *terrasse*[7] in Saint-Germain des Prés.

And with elegance the waiter asked, *"...vous désirez?"*[8]

Lunch in Paris is never a rushed event.

Being gourmand is time well spent!

Tartare, onion soup and croque-monsieur to start.

You'll order crème brulée, profiteroles and tarte tatin if you're smart.

[7]*Patio* | [8]*What would you like?*

RUE
GUILLAUME APOLLINAIRE
Le Bonaparte
RESTAURANT
- Vous Désirez ?

Once again we are off. Where will we end up next?

Just follow this Maman, because she knows best.

Down a narrow, cobbled road that lasted forever

Maman thought up an idea that was extra clever.

CAFE
BAR
STUDIO GALANDE
Le Marché FRANCE

Jardin des Tuileries was our next destination
to sail little boats in the perfect location.

Maman sits down to take in the view.
The children play till their next *rendez-vous.*[9]

Le Parisien

CHANEL

Paris is a city we all adore.

Where there is beauty, fashion and shopping galore.

We pass by Chanel, Dior and Celine to name a few.

All nestled together on the most luxurious avenue.

Avenue Montaigne is this *très chic*[10] Maman's heaven.

The Chanel bag in the window is her number one obsession!

[10]*Very stylish*

31
CHANEL
CHAN

Everything Maman wears is timeless and chic

From her little black dress to the slingback shoes on her feet.

But today Maman is shopping for baby.

Dior or Bonpoint, which will she fancy?

Floral romper, *bonnet,*[11] tiny socks with derby shoes.

Please don't forget a soft *doudou!*[12]

[11]Cap | [12]Cuddly toy

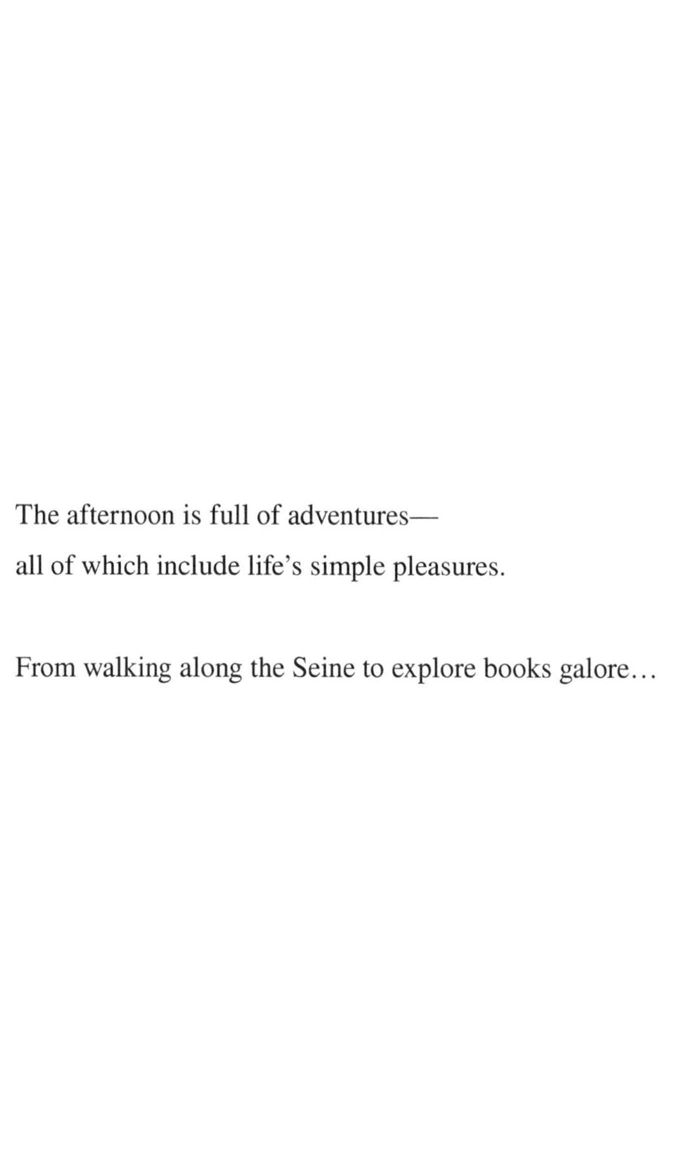

The afternoon is full of adventures—
all of which include life's simple pleasures.

From walking along the Seine to explore books galore…

VOGUE
VOGUE
Le Parisien
Le Parisien
Le Parisien
Le Petit Journal
Le Petit Jo
Le Petit Journal

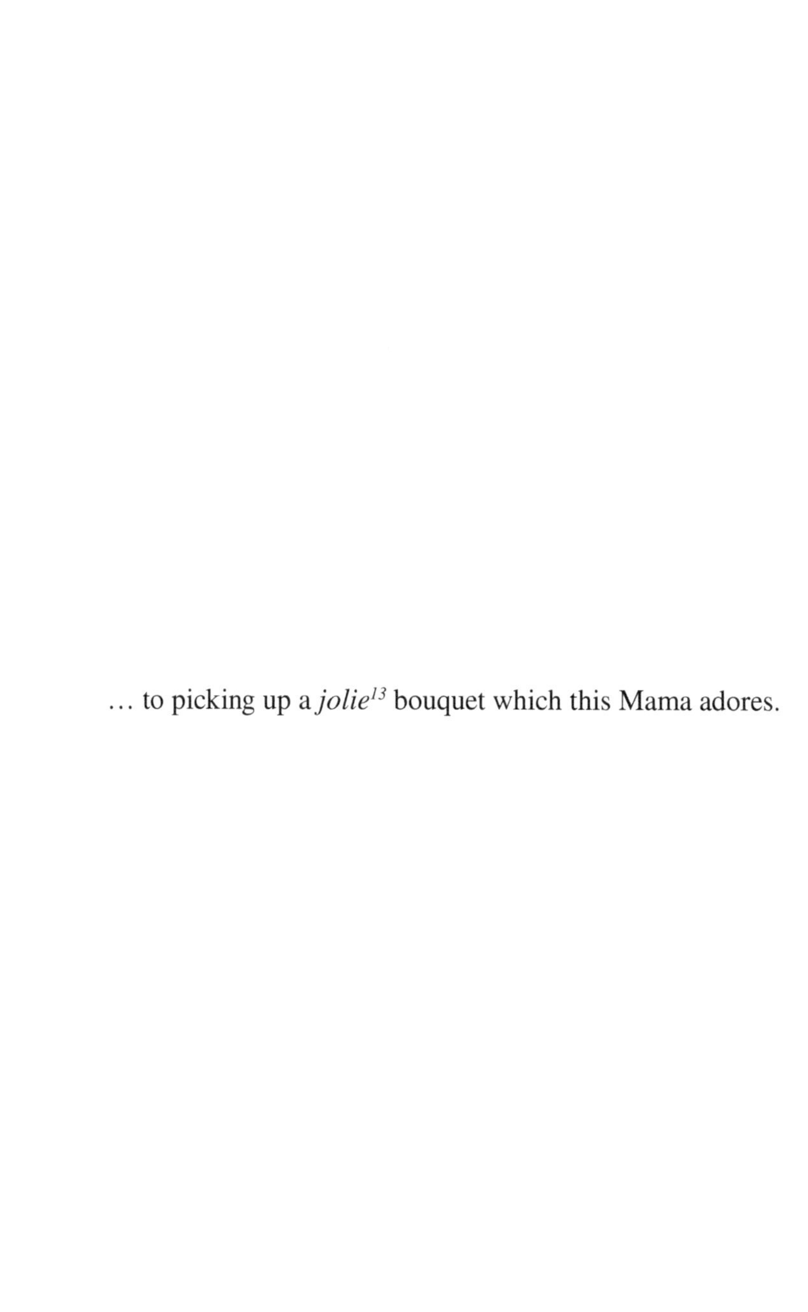

… to picking up a *jolie*[13] bouquet which this Mama adores.

[13]*Pretty*

FLEURS DE PRESTIGE
ouvert

L'après-midi[14] ends with *le goûter.*[15]

The children are hungry from this very long day.

The Sacre-Coeur is the perfect background for an afternoon snack.

Let's see what goodies Maman has packed!

Compote,[16] biscuits and *pain au lait*[17] - we want all three!

All from our local boulangerie!

[14]*Afternoon* | [15]*Snack* | [16]*Applesauce* | [17]*Milk bread*

LA SOIRÉE

It is evening in Paris. What will we do?

Stroll by the Louvre Pyramids for a phenomenal view!

As the sun starts to set, the lights start to glitter,

but nothing sparkles more than the two Parisian sisters.

It would be the perfect time to see a marionnette show

On the Champs-Elysees the puppet waves "hello!"

THEATRE
VRAI GVIGNOLET
Bonjour!

And just like magic as we exit the show

the terrasses come to life, it's the hour of the apéro![18]

We ride our bikes past tables full of olives, cornichons and chips

"Bon[19] apéro!" exclaims Maman who is in very good spirits.

Bar du Marché
Bar du Marché
Bar du Marché

In the distance we hear children laughing,

so we make our way over to see what is happening.

All lit up is a *carrousel*[20] going round and round.

What a hidden treasure we have found!

The children climb aboard for the last ride of the evening.

They whistle and sing as they go spinning and spinning.

[20]*Merry-go-round*

Je t'aime

Suddenly we realize our tummies are rumbling,

and notice that all of the brasserie's are bustling.

Cafe de Flore is iconic and charming.

An intimate setting with the best people watching.

Café de Flore
CAFE   FLORE

For dinner we order *blanquette de veau*[21]

and our Maman's favorite...yuck! *Escargots!!*[22]

The city is alive with light and never goes to sleep,

But this Maman and little ones are ready to rest their feet.

We cross Pont Alexandre III to head back home

In the distance we admire the Grand Palais dome.

Our *petit*[23] apartment is finally in sight
Maman picks up her sleepy little girl with all of her might.

Through the courtyard and up the winding staircase
We have arrived *chez nous,*[24] our happy place.

Maman tucks in the children and shuts the shutters.

Kisses foreheads goodnight and begins to mutter...

"Paris is a dream, *très*[24] charming and *mervielleux*[25]

but Maman thinks it would be nothing without you..."

[24]Very | [25]Marvelous

About the Author

Nicole Jarecz is a Detroit based fashion artist. She received her BFA in Illustration from the College for Creative Studies in Detroit, Michigan in 2010. Nicole has illustrated for some of the most luxurious fashion brands from around the world, such as Dior, Louis Vuitton, Tiffany & Co., Jimmy Choo, Roger Vivier, Saks Fifth Avenue and Gucci.

"Maman et Moi" was inspired by Nicole's experience of becoming a first time mom and living abroad in Paris, France from 2010 to 2015. She quickly fell in love with the many simple pleasures and *"joie de vivre"* of the French lifestyle.

The book merges her love of art, fashion and being a *"Maman"* in the City of Lights.

"Maman et Moi" is her first book.

Follow Nicole's adventures on Instagram
@nicolejareczillustration